Sharing

by Sam Williams

Content Consultant:
Melissa Z. Pierce, L.C.S.W.

Rourke
Educational Media

rourkeeducationalmedia.com

www.rourkeeducationalmedia.com

Dedication: To Michelle-for the adventures and friendship! Sam

Melissa Z. Pierce is a licensed clinical social worker with a background in counseling in the home and school group settings. Melissa is currently a life coach. She brings her experience as a L.C.S.W. and parent to the *Little World Social Skills* collection and the *Social Skills and More* program.

PHOTO CREDITS: Cover: © wavebreakmedia ltd; page 3: © Goldmund Lukic; page 5: © Chris Bernard; page 7: © Monkey Business Images; page 9: © Monkey Business Images; page 11: © Christopher Futcher; page 13: © Chris Bernard; page 15: © Christopher Futcher; page 17: © Christopher Futcher; page 19: © Darrin Henry; page 20: © Dmitriy Shironosov; page 23: ©Photos.com (glove and ball)

Illustrations by: Anita DuFalla

Edited by: Precious McKenzie

Cover and Interior designed by: Tara Raymo

Library of Congress PCN Data

Sharing / Sam Williams
(Little World Social Skills)
ISBN 978-1-61810-131-0 (hard cover)(alk. paper)
ISBN 978-1-61810-264-5 (soft cover)
ISBN 978-1-61810-390-1 (eBook)
ISBN 978-1-62717-372-8 (soft cover - Spanish)
ISBN 978-1-62717-556-2 (eBook - Spanish)
Library of Congress Control Number: 2011945275

Also Available as:

Rourke Educational Media
Printed in the United States of America,
North Mankato, Minnesota

Rourke
Educational Media

rourkeeducationalmedia.com

customerservice@rourkeeducationalmedia.com • PO Box 643328 Vero Beach, Florida 32964

Sharing means you use things together or take **turns**.

You can **share** things with your **family**.

How do you share with your family?

5

You can share your video game.

When your friends come over, you can share snacks with them.

You can share **equipment** with your **team.**

You can share crayons with your classmates so everyone can get their work done.

13

You can share when you **play** at the park.

We take turns.

15

You can share your seat when you ride the bus.

What are some other ways you share every day?

What Would You Do...

If you had a toy that everyone wanted to play with?

If you saw someone not sharing?

If you were playing a board game and your friend wasn't taking turns?

Picture Glossary

 **equipment** (i-KWIP-muhnt): The tools you need to do something.

 **family** (FAM-uh-lee): A group of people related to one another.

 **play** (play): To take part in a game.

share (shair):
To use something together.

team (teem):
A group of people who work or play together.

turns (turnz):
Chances to do something.

Index

Websites

www.kidsource.com
www.naeyc.com
www.drjean.org

About the Author

Sam Williams lives with his two dogs, Abby and Cooper, in Florida. Cooper is very good about sharing his toys with Abby.

Meet The Author!
www.meetREMauthors.com